FAULT LINES

JOHN PERRITANO

red rhino
b**OO**ks®
NONFICTION

SADDLEBACK
EDUCATIONAL PUBLISHING
www.sdlback.com

Photo credits: page 33: Garry Gay Photography / Alamy.com; page 35: Aurora Photos / Alamy.com; page 45: ersoy emin / Alamy.com; All other source images from Shutterstock.com

ISBN-13: 978-1-68021-053-8
ISBN-10: 1-68021-053-X
eBook: 978-1-63078-372-3

Printed in Malaysia

21 20 19 18 17   3 4 5 6 7

TABLE OF CONTENTS

Chapter 1
MOMENT OF TERROR

A small town in California.
A boy and girl are at home.
Their mom ran to the store.

There is a rumble.
The house shakes.
A little at first.
Then it rocks.
The ceiling falls.
Dishes break.
It is an earthquake.
A big one.

The boy thinks.
They have drills at school.
Earthquake drills.
He takes his sister's hand.
They go under a table.
Just in time.
The house falls.
They are buried.

The shaking stops.
The boy and girl are alive.
But they are trapped.

People rush to help.
They dig.
Move bricks.
Move wood.
They work day and night.

It takes two days.

At last, a crack of light.

It pours into the dark hole.

The hole opens wide.

An arm reaches in.

Then another.

Rescuers.

They pull the girl out.

The boy is next.

Cheers ring out.

The boy and girl are lucky.
People were ready.
Why?
Their town sits on a *fault line*.
One of the big ones.

Chapter 2
THE EARTH'S CORE

We live on Earth's surface.

But there is a lot we don't see.

Our planet is made of layers.

The first is the core.

Earth's center.

It is mostly metal.

Iron.

Nickel.

Both are elements.

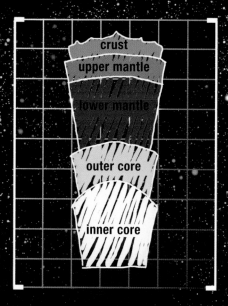

The core has two parts.

The outer part is hot.

Almost as hot as the sun.

It is so hot rock melts.

The inner part is hotter.

But it is solid.

Why?

The outer core is heavy.

It pushes on the inner core.

That's a lot of pressure.

It keeps the inner rock from melting.

The _____ is the second layer.
It covers the core.
Mantle rock is soft.

It moves slowly.

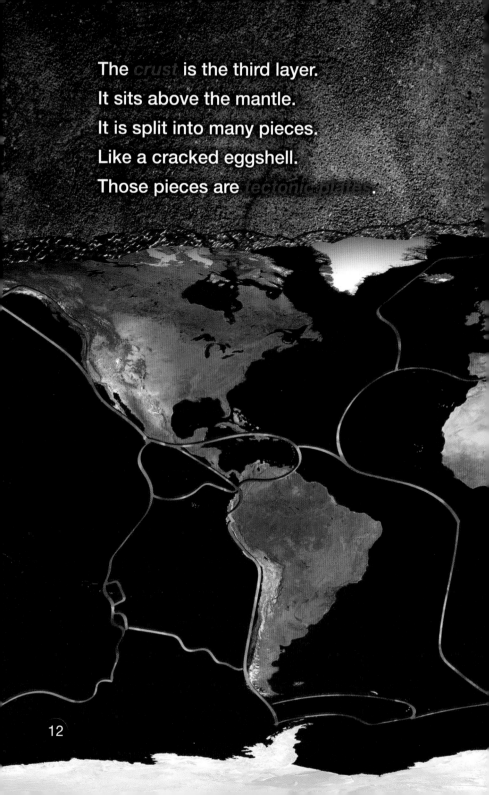

The crust is the third layer.
It sits above the mantle.
It is split into many pieces.
Like a cracked eggshell.
Those pieces are tectonic plates.

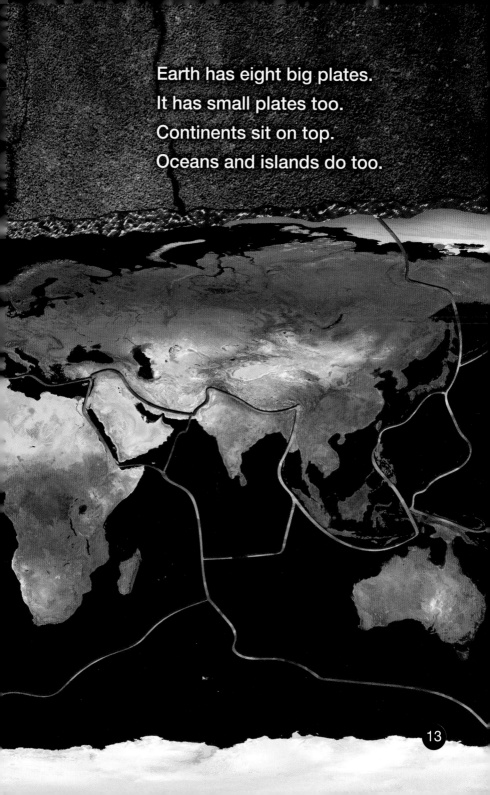

Earth has eight big plates.
It has small plates too.
Continents sit on top.
Oceans and islands do too.

These plates float on the mantle.

They move just a bit each year.

About three inches.

That's as fast as your fingernails grow.

The plates are like bumper cars.

They bump into each other.

Rock grinds.

That makes cracks in the crust.

We call these cracks fault lines.

Earth shakes when faults move.

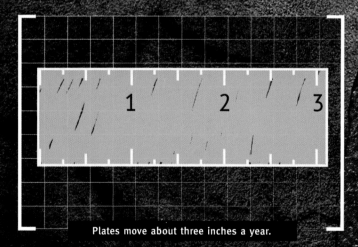

Plates move about three inches a year.

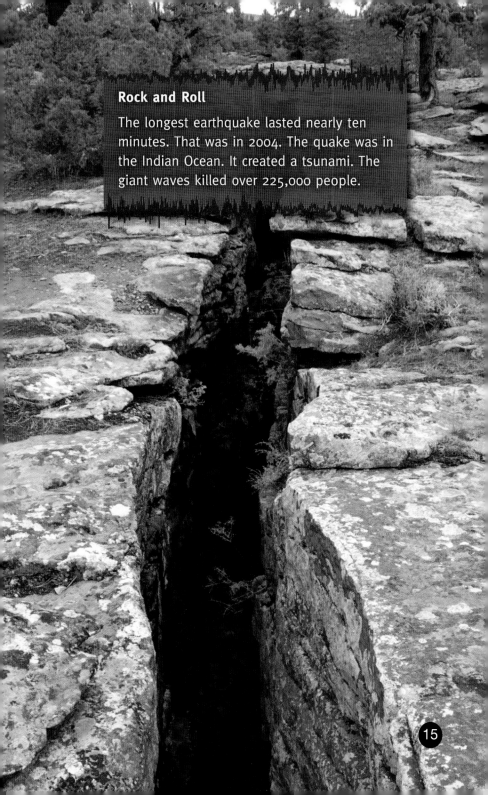

Rock and Roll

The longest earthquake lasted nearly ten minutes. That was in 2004. The quake was in the Indian Ocean. It created a tsunami. The giant waves killed over 225,000 people.

Chapter 3
FINDING FAULT

Some faults are thin and short.
They can be as thin as a human hair.
Others go on for miles.
Some are near the surface.
Others are below ground.
Some you can see.
Others you can't.

Most faults happen where
tectonic plates meet.
Most earthquakes occur there too.

Surface crack of the San Andreas fault after the 1906 San Francisco earthquake.

There are three main faults.

Strike-slip.

They form when rocks pass each other.

Thrust.

They form when rocks slide up.

Normal.

They form when rocks slide down.

Rock and Roll

The biggest fault lines are hundreds of miles long. They can be seen from space.

Time is an earthquake's best friend.
Pressure builds along the faults.
Slowly.
Steadily.
Then the rocks move.
They split.

They shift.
Kaboom!
They let go of energy.
A lot of energy.
It shakes the planet.

Chapter 4
WHAT IS A HOTSPOT?

Earthquakes shake things up.

They can cause damage.

Some cause a lot.

People want to be ready.

But that is not always possible.

It helps to know about fault lines.

They are earthquake hotspots.

Think of the tectonic plates.

Some bump against each other a lot.

Ever heard of the Ring of Fire?

It is an earthquake hotspot.

Nine out of ten quakes happen there.

Damage done by an earthquake off the coast of Chile.

Ring of Fire

The Ring of Fire is not one fault line.

It is many.

The Pacific Plate is in the ring's center.

It rubs against other plates.

All in or next to the Pacific Ocean.

The Ring hugs the U.S. West Coast.

South America. Japan. China.

Southeast Asia. Australia.

The quakes can be powerful.

One happened in Alaska.

It was the strongest quake to shake the U.S.

Epicenter of the **Great Alaskan Earthquake in 1964.**

Scientists study fault lines.
They *monitor* hotspots.
We call these scientists *seismologists*.
They measure earthquakes.
How?

Each earthquake has a *focus*.
That's where the shaking starts.
It is usually underground.
Each quake also has an *epicenter*.
This is a point on the surface.
It is right above the focus.

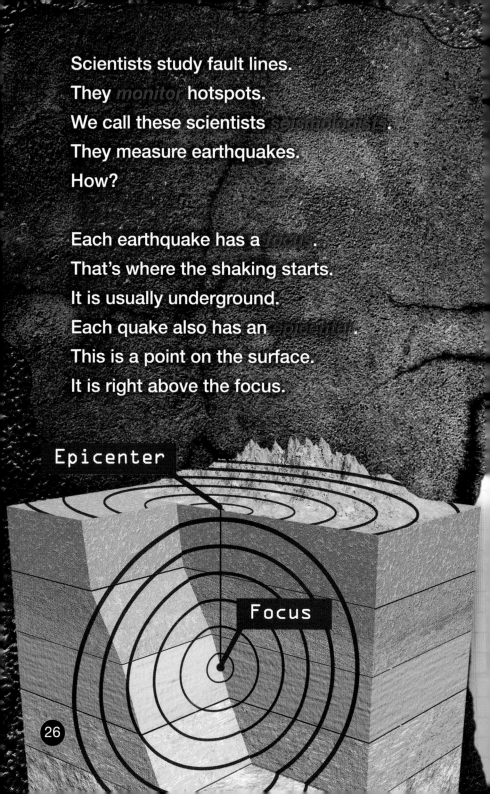

Epicenter

Focus

26

Energy moves from the focus in waves.

Seismic waves.

Shock waves.

Scientists use a special machine.

A *seismograph*.

It measures shock waves.

It figures out a quake's power.

27

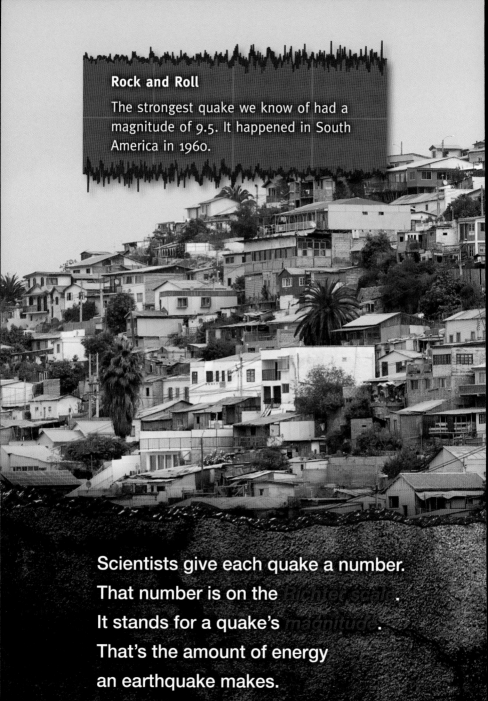

Rock and Roll

The strongest quake we know of had a magnitude of 9.5. It happened in South America in 1960.

Scientists give each quake a number.
That number is on the *Richter scale*.
It stands for a quake's *magnitude*.
That's the amount of energy
an earthquake makes.

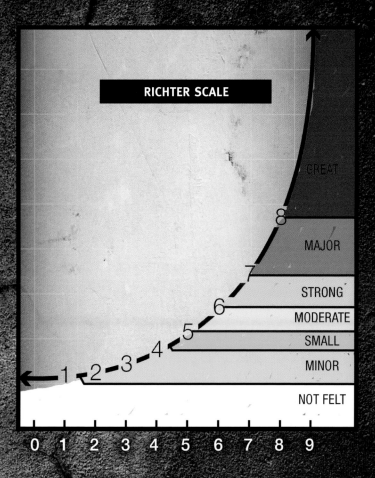

RICHTER SCALE

GREAT

MAJOR

STRONG

MODERATE

SMALL

MINOR

NOT FELT

0 1 2 3 4 5 6 7 8 9

The Richter scale begins at zero.

It doesn't end.

The smaller the number.

The weaker the quake.

The higher the number.

The stronger the quake.

Fault lines are a big help.

They show us where quakes will be.

But what about when?

Scientists can only guess.

Some try to predict.

They use tools.

A special seismograph.

It looks for changes in seismic waves.

The changes may be small.

But they mean big things.

A fault is getting weak.

A quake may occur.

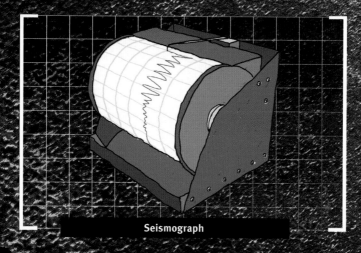

Seismograph

Scientists want to keep people safe.

The worst quakes are called "Big Ones."

The superquakes.

No one knows when a Big One will occur.

But scientists have a good idea where.

The hottest hotspots.

Fault lines that see the most action.

Chapter 5
HOTSPOT NO. 1

SAN ANDREAS FAULT

October 17, 1989.

San Francisco, California.

Baseball fans crowded into

Candlestick Park.

It was Game 3 of the World Series.

Millions watched on TV.

An earthquake rumbled.

The stadium shook.

TV screens went blank.

The quake rattled for 15 seconds.
Short.
Powerful.
A magnitude 6.9 quake.
Homes were destroyed.
Bridges buckled.
More than 60 people died.
Thousands more were hurt.
The San Andreas Fault had moved.

The San Andreas Fault runs through California.
It sits on one side of the Ring of Fire.
Two plates meet here.
The Pacific Plate.
And the North American Plate.

The fault is 600 miles long.
You can see it.
You can walk on it.
This fault is an earthquake machine.
It is to blame for 20 major quakes.
One almost destroyed San Francisco.
That was in 1906.
Thousands died.

The San Andreas is a strike-slip fault.
Its sides scrape together.
Scientists fear another major quake
on the fault.
The Big One.
It will be worse than the 1989 quake.
More powerful than the 1906 quake.
A magnitude 8 or greater.

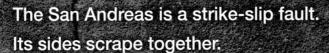

Fact or Fiction?

An earthquake will force California to fall into the ocean.

Fiction: California borders two plates. They slide past each other. North to South. The state will not fall into the ocean. But Los Angeles will one day be near San Francisco.

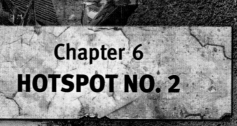

Chapter 6
HOTSPOT NO. 2

LONGMEN SHAN FAULT

May 12, 2008.

Sichuan, China.

Students were studying.

Workers were at their jobs.

Shoppers were shopping.

A violent quake rocked the city.

A magnitude 7.9 quake.

It shook for two minutes.

Buildings snapped.

Brick huts turned to dust.

70,000 died.
Thousands were hurt.
The epicenter was 12 miles below ground.
The Longmen Shan Fault had split.

Longmen Shan borders two plates.

The Indian Plate is one.

It pushes north.

It moves over the Eurasian Plate.

That makes it a thrust fault.

Big quakes happen here.

One killed 9,300 people in 1933.

The fault worries scientists.

They know large quakes will happen again.

Magnitude 7.7 or more.

One may happen in the next 50 years.

Chapter 7

HOTSPOT NO. 3

NEW MADRID FAULT

Missouri. 1811 and 1812.

Earthquakes hit the area.

One was very big.

A magnitude 8.

The ground rose.

Trees fell.

Waves tossed boats from the

Mississippi River.

They landed on the shore.

The New Madrid Fault had moved.

No one died.

Not many lived there then.

New Madrid is not like most faults.

It's far from where plates meet.

Scientists are sure it will move again.

It will be a big quake.

Like last time.

More deadly too.

Millions now live in the area.

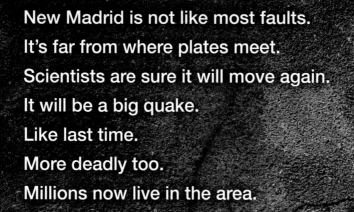

Rock and Roll

The biggest earthquake along the New Madrid Fault was on February 7, 1812. People on boats said the Mississippi River ran backward for hours after the quake.

St. Louis

Mississippi River

Memphis

Chapter 8
HOTSPOT NO. 4

ALASKA-ALEUTIAN FAULT

March 27, 1964.

Alaska.

A big quake hit off the coast.

A magnitude 9.2.

The ground rose 38 feet in some places.

It dipped seven feet in others.

Then a *tsunami* came ashore.

A deadly wall of water.

It was created by the quake.

Its waves were 220 feet high.

128 people died.

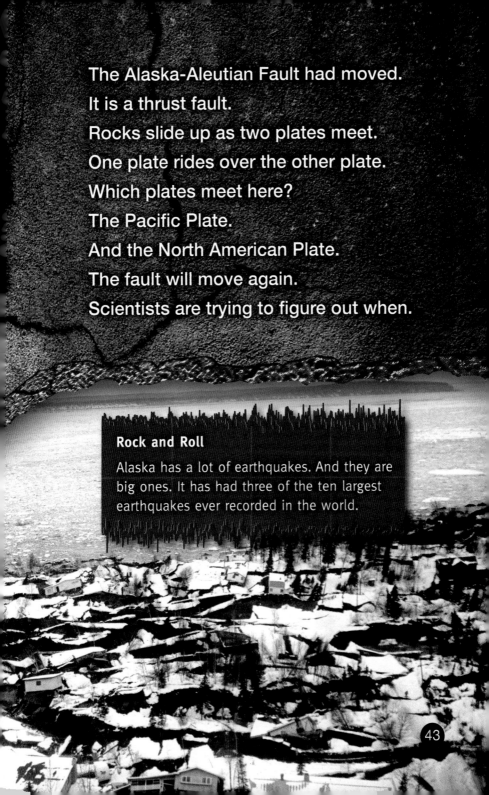

The Alaska-Aleutian Fault had moved.

It is a thrust fault.

Rocks slide up as two plates meet.

One plate rides over the other plate.

Which plates meet here?

The Pacific Plate.

And the North American Plate.

The fault will move again.

Scientists are trying to figure out when.

Rock and Roll

Alaska has a lot of earthquakes. And they are big ones. It has had three of the ten largest earthquakes ever recorded in the world.

NORTH ANATOLIAN FAULT

August 17, 1999.

Northwest Turkey.

A country in Asia.

A magnitude 7.6 quake.

It killed 17,000 people.

The North Anatolian Fault gave way.

It is a strike-slip fault.

600 miles long.

And it is active.

The Anatolian Plate is always on the move.

It sits between two plates.

The Arabian Plate.

And the Eurasian Plate.

They squeeze the Anatolian Plate.

The fault has split many times.

Some quakes were larger than magnitude 7.

People worry.

A monster quake could kill many here.

14 million people live in Turkey's capital.

Chapter 10
BRACING FOR THE BIG ONE

Earthquakes.

We can't stop them.

We can't predict them.

But fault lines give us a clue.

We know where they might hit.

We can prepare.

How?

We can build things better.

Bridges. Workplaces. Homes.

We can use "smart" materials.

They can withstand most shaking.

They're better than steel.

Stronger than concrete.

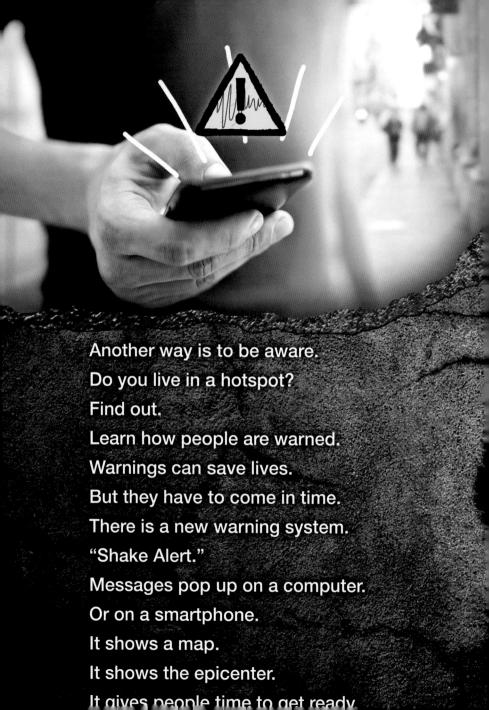

Another way is to be aware.
Do you live in a hotspot?
Find out.
Learn how people are warned.
Warnings can save lives.
But they have to come in time.
There is a new warning system.
"Shake Alert."
Messages pop up on a computer.
Or on a smartphone.
It shows a map.
It shows the epicenter.
It gives people time to get ready.

You can do things to stay safe.

Stay inside.

Make a survival kit.

Water. Food. Flashlights. Batteries.

Keep away from the ocean.

Earthquakes can cause big waves.

Keep away from electric wires.

They can fall in a quake.

Know which fault line is closest to you.

And be ready.

We never know when a quake will hit.

GLOSSARY

core: center

crust: the top layer of Earth

elements: materials that cannot be chemically broken down into simpler pieces

epicenter: the point on Earth's surface directly above where an earthquake starts

fault line: a break or crack in Earth's crust

focus: the point where an earthquake begins

hotspot: a place with more activity or action

iron: a heavy metal that is very common

magnitude: the number that shows the power of an earthquake

mantle: the middle layer of Earth

molten: changed into liquid by heat

monitor: to watch or check for something

nickel: a hard metal that is silver-white

pressure: the force made when something presses or pushes against something else

Richter scale: a scale that measures the strength of an earthquake

seismic wave: an invisible wave of energy that moves through the ground

seismograph: a machine that records the movement of the ground during an earthquake

seismologist: a scientist who studies earthquakes

tectonic plates: rocky parts of Earth's crust that move

tsunami: a very large wave in the ocean usually caused by an earthquake

TAKE A LOOK INSIDE

GREAT SPIES of the WORLD

She puts in a memory stick.
Begins to copy the file.
She's not a *traitor*.
That's what she tells herself.
But she needs money.
So she has to steal secrets.

Footsteps.
She looks up.
A guard is checking the doors.
Her heart races.
The file finishes downloading.
The plans are hers.
She ducks under the desk.
Time ticks by.
The guard passes.
That was close.
Too close.

Chapter 2
I SPY

Spies steal secrets.
From whom?
Governments.
The military.
Businesses.

Spying is called *espionage*.
It is about getting *information*.
Things few know about.
Maps.
Battle plans.
Secret weapons.
Letters.

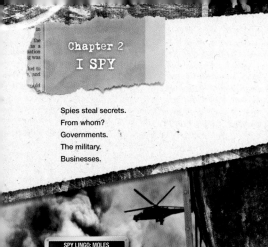

SPY LINGO: MOLES
Some spies are called moles.
Moles are animals. They hide
and dig in the ground. Spies
dig for secrets. They hide too.

Chapter 5
TONY MENDEZ: SCI-FI SPY

Iran.
A country in the Middle East.
1979.
The U.S. was a friend of Iran's leader.
His people did not like him.
They pushed him out of power.
He came to the U.S.
That made many people mad.

PASSPORT
UNITED STATES MISSION
TEHRAN, IRAN

IDENTIFICATION ORDER
NO. 76492

NAME: Tony Mendez

SPY FOR: United States

TIME PERIOD: 1979

A mob circled the U.S. *embassy*.
It was in Tehran.
Iran's capital.
They stormed the building.
They took *hostages*.
Six escaped.
Canadians hid them.
But they could not do it for long.
The Americans had to find a way out.

9781680210378

9781680210286

9781680210309

9781680210507

9781680210354

9781680210521

9781680210361

9781680210323

9781680210330

MORE TITLES COMING SOON